TRIBAL REVOLUTIONARY

BIRSA MUNDA

TUHIN A. SINHA
PRESENTS

TRIBAL REVOLUTIONARY

BIRSA MUNDA

WRITTEN BY
SUNITA PANT BANSAL

KONARK

Konark Publishers Pvt. Ltd
206, First Floor,
Peacock Lane, Shahpur Jat,
New Delhi - 110 049
+91-11-4105 5065
india@konarkpublishers.com, us@konarkpublishers.com
www.konarkpublishers.com

Copyright © Sunita Pant Bansal, 2025

All rights reserved. No part of this book may be reproduced or utilised in any form or by any means, electronic or mechanical, including photocopying, recording, or by any information storage and retrieval system, without prior written permission from the author or the publisher. The views and opinions expressed in this book are solely those of the author and the presenter. While the accuracy of the facts, as reported by the author and the presenter, has been verified to the fullest extent possible, the publisher is not liable in any way for the content.

ISBN: 978-81-973432-0-9

Edited by Ranjana Narayan
Jacket design by Sourish Mitra
Chapter illustrations © Freepik & Pixabay
Illustrations by Jitendra Kumar Patra
Chapter design by Pramod Kumar
Typeset by Saanvi Graphics, Noida
Printed and bound at Thomson Press (India) Ltd

To the memory of Birsa Munda and other tribal heroes whose immense courage and supreme sacrifice played a crucial role in giving momentum to the Indian Independence movement.

CONTENTS

Introduction by Tuhin A. Sinha	ix
1. Birsa is Born	1
2. Early Years	13
3. Awakening to Injustice	23
4. The Search	30
5. Learning and Introspection	34
6. Going Home	42
7. A Call to Action	54
8. Birsa is Imprisoned	63

9.	Birsa is Released	69
10.	Preparations for the Uprising	73
11.	Call for Rebellion	78
12.	The Uprising	86
13.	The Beginning of the End	95
14.	Birsa's Arrest and Final Days	101
15.	Birsa's Legacy	106
	References	112

Introduction

As the nation gears up to celebrate the 150th birth anniversary of Birsa Munda, there is an unprecedented surge in interest surrounding this iconic hero. Birsa Munda, a tribal revolutionary whose legacy was once relegated to the margins of history, is now receiving the attention he truly deserves. This resurgence of Birsa Munda's legacy is a testament to the growing recognition of the sacrifices made by our subaltern heroes and freedom fighters.

A significant catalyst in this renewed awareness has been Prime Minister Narendra Modi's constant references to Birsa Munda. Through his speeches and public engagements, PM Modi has invoked Birsa Munda's spirit and sacrifices, using his story to inspire and mobilize the youth of India.

For me, Birsa Munda's story is more than just a

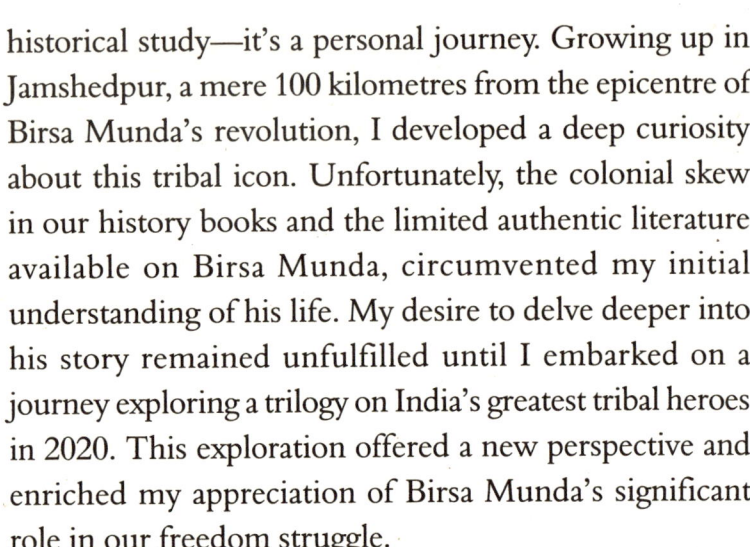

historical study—it's a personal journey. Growing up in Jamshedpur, a mere 100 kilometres from the epicentre of Birsa Munda's revolution, I developed a deep curiosity about this tribal icon. Unfortunately, the colonial skew in our history books and the limited authentic literature available on Birsa Munda, circumvented my initial understanding of his life. My desire to delve deeper into his story remained unfulfilled until I embarked on a journey exploring a trilogy on India's greatest tribal heroes in 2020. This exploration offered a new perspective and enriched my appreciation of Birsa Munda's significant role in our freedom struggle.

On 15 August 2023, I had the opportunity to visit Ulihatu, the birthplace of Birsa Munda. The experience was both enlightening and a bit disheartening. Meeting the villagers, including two of Birsa Munda's descendants, I was struck by the condition of the village and the lack of awareness about Birsa Munda's struggles among the locals, many of whom have converted to Christianity. This visit reinforced my resolve to amplify the teachings of Birsa Munda's life among the poor children of the community.

When Sunita Pant Bansal proposed writing a foundational level book on Birsa Munda, I was thrilled to support this initiative. Sunita's book promises to present Birsa Munda's story in a lucid and engaging manner, making it assimilative and engaging to young readers.

Her work is a significant step towards ensuring that Birsa Munda's life and contributions are well understood and appreciated by the next generation.

One of our primary goals in this endeavour is to push for the inclusion of this book in school curricula in states that are connected to Birsa Munda's legacy. We believe that understanding his extraordinary life—marked by numerous transformations and unparalleled sacrifices—can provide valuable lessons for students across the country.

I would like to extend my heartfelt gratitude to Konark Publishers and Sunita Pant Bansal for their dedication and hard work. It is high time we honour our real heroes—those who have long been unsung yet played a crucial role in defending Bharat Mata and Sanatan Dharma.

I hope that readers will find this journey through Birsa Munda's life as enriching and inspiring as I have. His story is a beacon of courage and resilience, and it is our collective responsibility to ensure that his legacy continues to inspire and educate future generations.

Jai Hind!

Mumbai **Tuhin A. Sinha**

1
Birsa is Born

Hundreds of years ago, two tribal brothers Chutu Haram and Nagu along with their friends set out to find a permanent place to build their homes. On reaching the banks of river Domtamara (Damodar), the boys were amazed by the natural beauty on the other side of the river. It seemed like an ideal place to settle down with their families!

However, crossing the river to explore the other side was a huge challenge. There were no boats, the strong flow of the water was dangerous for swimming, and the river was deep. The boys could not simply wade across!

While they stood trying to figure a way out, Chutu spotted a large wooden log floating close to the bank. He quickly slithered down the slippery ground, and jumping into the water, held on to the log with all his might. The others followed.

Finally, the boys managed to reach the other side. Tired and soaked to the bone, they clambered up the riverbank, dragging the log behind them. Just then, one of the boys spotted a tiny mouse peeping out from one of the holes in the log!

The presence of the mouse was considered auspicious by the tribals. The boys were convinced that this divine tract of land was chosen by the gods for them. The decision was taken! The boys and their families came down to settle there.

Since Chutu had brought them there, the place began to be known as Chutia. Those of the Purti clan who settled there were called Chutia Purti, and their successors

were called Mundas. Owing to the names Chutu Haram and Nagu, the place ultimately became Chota Nagpur.

As word spread, people from surrounding areas too came to settle down in this beautiful place. Not all of them were tribals. The population started increasing steadily, of tribals as well as non-tribals.

The Munda tribal community lived in the open initially. But with the increasing population of non-tribals, they were forced to restrict their movement, and later were compelled to move out and seek shelter elsewhere. Some of these tribals moved to Ulihatu. Among them was Lakari Munda.

Sugna Munda, son of Lakari Munda, got married to Karmi, daughter of Dibar Munda. The couple had five children, Komta, Daskir, Champa, Birsa and Kanu.

This is the extraordinary story of the extraordinary boy, Birsa.

In the heart of the Chota Nagpur plateau, where the earth met the sky in an eternal embrace, lay the serene village of Ulihatu. It was a place of natural beauty, where the rhythm of life followed the cycles of nature, and the ancient tribal traditions were an important part of existence.

It was here, amidst the rustling leaves and babbling brooks, in a thatched hut, on a moonlit night, that a beautiful little baby was born to Karmi. Sugna, the proud father of the baby, named him Birsa. It was Thursday, 15 November 1875.

Birsa's birth was heralded by an aura of mystique. Legend has it that the forest seemed to whisper secrets of greatness as the newborn cried his first cries. Some villagers claimed to see a comet moving across the night sky in the direction from Chalkad to Ulihatu. Others saw a flag fluttering on a distant hilltop.

A halo-like divine light seemed to bathe the baby boy. The elders of the village saw in him a spark, a fire that would ignite the spirit of their oppressed community.

Sugna and Karmi, the proud parents, looked upon their newborn son with awe and wonder. In his tiny form, they saw the promise of a bright future, a future filled with hope and possibility. Little did they know, their son would go beyond their imagination! Birsa would grow up to become a beacon of light in the darkest of times, a leader whose name would be etched in the annals of history.

Those were the days of the British Raj

in India. To control different parts of the vast country, the British administration had empowered the landlords to earn revenue for them. Unfortunately, the landlords had become greedy and misused their power to torture the poor farmers.

The Mundas were farmers. They were made to work hard by the landlords but were denied the use of the village well, as they were tribals, considered the lowest in the caste hierarchy of the land. The poor tribals were illiterate and the landlords believed that they were sent by God to serve the higher castes. The situation was so bad that some tribals did not even have the means to have two meals a day. The Mundas had no choice but to continue tolerating the injustice.

Sugna was no different. But somehow, the birth of Birsa changed something in him.

From the moment of his birth, Birsa seemed to possess a quiet strength and determination that belied his age. Unlike other babies, he did not cry much and smiled at everyone. His eyes, wide and curious, took in the world around him with a sense of wonder, as if he were already aware of the great destiny that lay ahead for him.

Sugna felt he owed it to Birsa to protect him from the kind of life he himself lived.

Meanwhile, Christian missionaries had begun to spread in the country. Though they were religious preachers, their aim was to strengthen the grip of the British administration in India, by targeting the poor and the weak. Constant exploitation by the privileged had reduced the poor to utter wretchedness. This widening gap between the rich and the poor was used as a tool by the British through their Christian missionaries.

The missionaries went to the poor, emphasised the issue of exploitation, and promised all assistance to end their woes.

"What has your religion given you? Poverty, hunger and deprivation. On the contrary, Christianity can give you everything that is till now limited to the upper class."

Slowly the idea began to seep in and the tribals began to adopt Christianity. Though Sugna also belonged to the deprived class and was exploited by the landlords, he had not succumbed to the missionaries, yet.

Sugna had faith in his own self and in his land. He just had to work harder to feed his growing family. But no, it was not that simple! Unknown to Sugna, destiny had very different plans for him.

His life turned around completely when the British administration declared a new law under which the tribals could no longer own or cultivate the forest land around their village. Even their animals could not graze beyond the limits of the village. The law stated that all the land belonged to the landlord and the tribals were his employees. They would get salaries but would have to pay rent to the landlord.

This was a huge blow to the Mundas. Until then they were only coping up with the landlord's exploitation, but now they had lost everything. Their lands, their forests were not theirs anymore!

"What kind of a hopeless world will our children grow up in!" Sugna wondered in despair.

In the background of the spreading Christianity, would Sugna have to give up his ancestral cultural values, his identity, and adopt a way of life that was entirely alien to who he was? This recurring concern had started to weigh heavily on him.

Sugna still did not lose hope. His back-breaking work kept him away from his family and barely provided one meal a day for them. But seeing the smiling cherubic face of his toddler son Birsa on reaching home would make Sugna forget all his misery.

His wife Karmi never complained. But one night, she could not bear to see her husband suffer so much. She suggested that their eldest son, 10-year-old Komta, should help.

"Whatever little money Komta will earn will ease your burden," Karmi gently suggested to Sugna.

Though not entirely whole-heartedly, Sugna agreed, and Komta took up a menial job in a rich household. Komta's wages helped the family get two meals a day.

Birsa was growing up to be a bright and jolly child. From the moment he could toddle, he eagerly explored the world around him. He learnt easily whatever his parents taught him.

Sugna and Karmi instilled in him a reverence for nature and a respect for the traditions of their Munda tribe. They taught him the names of the plants and animals that populated their surroundings, weaving stories of their significance into the fabric of his young mind.

"Come what may, I will not let my Birsa suffer the way we are suffering. I will do whatever it takes to give him a good life," Sugna promised himself.

Though Komta's support was helpful, Sugna still had to endure the increasing financial pressure from the landlord.

Even if the crops did not do well because of the weather, the landlord still had to be paid the revenue due from the land, which the British colonial administration increased at whim. Not only the tribal farmers toiled on the land which they had owned once and which had been snatched away from them, they had to pay rent for it too.

The only aim of the landlord was to earn money for his masters, the British administration. And the poor Mundas were often forced to borrow money at exorbitant rates from moneylenders who had begun flooding the region. These moneylenders were non-tribal outsiders. Under the patronage of the landlords and the British administration, they committed unthinkable atrocities upon the Mundas.

A deep sense of hopelessness began to take root in the village.

"We must be doing something wrong to be suffering

like this. How can a God we have been worshipping all our lives be so heartless? Where is He when our children are dying of starvation?" Such were the sentiments of Sugna's friends and fellow farmers.

A lot of them were heading towards conversion to Christianity, a religion that promised equality of people and giving equal opportunities for progress.

Sugna knew what he had to do when the time came… but not yet.

The proverbial straw that broke the camel's back hit Sugna hard one day when one of the moneylenders tried to attack his wife Karmi. It was then that he realised that the village was not safe anymore for his wife and children. There was no future for his family in such a place. He did not want his children to grow up with fear in their hearts.

Sugna decided to leave Ulihatu for good. He wanted to live in a place where his hard work would be appropriately rewarded. He did not want his children to experience any more hardships. He wanted them to be literate.

Karmi's cousin sister, Joni, lived in Bamba, a small village 250km away from Ulihatu. According to her, their landlord was not as ruthless and

exploitative as other landlords. So, life was slightly better for the farmers in Bamba.

Sugna and Karmi packed up their belongings, gathered their children, and walked away from Ulihatu, heading towards Bamba. Birsa was five years old then.

2
Early Years

Sugna, Karmi and their children settled down in Bamba. Life was better here because the landlord was good. He helped those in need and did not impose unnecessary fines or punish his workers at whim.

As time went on, Sugna saw the role Christian missionaries played in the lives of the villagers. He realised that converting to Christianity was likely to help him and his family in many ways. But at the same time, it also meant that they would have to worship a new God. They would have to assume a different cultural identity as well. The worst part was that they would have to support those who had uprooted them and taken over their homeland.

Sugna and Karmi would discuss this and get stuck on the point on whether conversion would guarantee a better life for their children. Ultimately, everything depended on that. As parents, they were willing to do anything, if it assured a better future for their children.

So, under the dark, looming shadow of conversion, Sugna and Karmi clung on to their Munda heritage and regaled a 6-year-old Birsa with legends and stories of their ancestral heroes. They taught him the ways of the Mundas—the rituals that honoured the spirits of the land, the traditional dances that celebrated the changing seasons, and the steadfast bond of community that held them all together. Little Birsa listened with rapt attention, absorbing everything.

Ultimately, the inevitable happened. One evening, Sugna met a Christian missionary who seemed very kind. Sugna couldn't help himself and listened to him.

He said, "Sugna, I am here to help you. I understand your plight. As tribals, the landlords will always treat you as their slaves. You will never be allowed to drink water from their wells or enter the temples. The upper class people have created divisions among people born on the same land. Your ancestors have tolerated this injustice for long. You have also tolerated. Your children will have to do the same. Don't you want to lead a respectable life? Don't you want your own land? Don't you want your children to grow up as educated and respectable people? Hindu religion will never allow you to do so, because it believes in upper and lower caste divisions. Whereas Christianity believes in equality of people and gives equal opportunities for progress to all. So, if you don't want any more hardship in your life, embrace Christianity."

The priest's gentle voice had the desired effect on Sugna.

"Once you embrace Isa Masih, you will be free from the caste system. The mission treats everyone as equal, and we will provide financial and medical help whenever you and your family need it. Your children will have a brighter future once they are in our care."

More than himself, Sugna was keen on ensuring a respectable life for his children. Respect could be earned only if they became educated. And that would be possible if they went to missionary schools. This was the deciding point!

Sugna adopted Christianity and came to be known as Masihdas.

The moment news of Sugna's conversion reached Karmi's sister Joni and their brother Sohrai, they came rushing over. Although Karmi and the children had not converted, still the two were quite upset.

"Do you really want to see Birsa wearing a cross, adopting a different name, and praying to a different God?" they asked Karmi.

"No! Of course not!" exclaimed Karmi. But she knew why Sugna did what he did. It was not an easy decision at all.

As luck would have it, Sugna's dream of the missionaries taking care of his children's education remained unfulfilled. Why?

Because the landlords of Bamba village did not want people from lower castes to be literate. They themselves had converted to Christianity and did not want their children to study with the tribal children.

The British had empowered the landlords, who reciprocated by pleasing the officers with precious gifts. As a result, no complaint against the landlords was ever registered and they continued to exploit the poor. The British were using the landlords to rule over the masses.

In such a situation, the missionaries did not want to displease the British administration by opposing the landlords. So, going back on their promise, they banned the entry of tribal children in schools.

This problem opened up an opportunity for little Birsa. Joni and Sohrai convinced Sugna and Karmi to let them take Birsa to their maternal village Ayubhatu. It was not yet influenced by Christian missionaries. The biggest advantage with Ayubhatu was Jaypal Nag's school, which was dedicated to educating tribal children.

Sugna and Karmi would not have parted with the child they loved the most so easily, but they understood that education was essential for Birsa to avoid the life he had led thus far.

Six-year-old Birsa's life took yet another turn when he went to Ayubhatu to live with his grandparents, uncle and aunt. There, he would acquire education without giving up his identity and cultural heritage.

Birsa took to this new phase of his life as fish to water. He loved the village school and looked forward to

attending classes every day. Unlike most children, who barely followed what the teachers taught, and who were more interested in whiling away time, Birsa would listen attentively to every word. He was quick to understand what was being taught, and no subject was difficult for him. He also had several questions to ask his teachers at the end of each lesson!

Birsa's love for learning was evident as his curiosity spilled out through questions. He was fascinated by the stories of *Ramayana* and *Mahabharata* that Jaypal Nag narrated during their last class every day. One day, he surprised his teacher by comparing the British administration and the landlords to Ravana!

Jaypal Nag was impressed to see Birsa connecting what he was hearing in class to what he was experiencing in life. He had seen many good students in his career, but Birsa was special. Nag knew that someday he would leave his mark on the entire society.

"Birsa is not an ordinary child," he told Joni. "He does not follow any lessons blindly, he thinks things over and reaches his own conclusions. See to it that he does not change."

Joni took Jaypal Nag's words to heart and became fiercely protective of Birsa.

Two years later, Joni got married. Her in-laws lived in a village called Khatanga, where she took Birsa along.

This sudden move to yet another new village did not agree well with Birsa. Within a short span of time, he had been uprooted from Ulihatu to Bamba, to Ayubhatu, to now Khatanga. He had been forced to leave behind everything familiar, his home, family and friends, all that gave him a sense of safety.

Birsa felt lost and lonely in his new surroundings.

Khatanga had recently been frequented by Christian missionaries. They were visiting homes, praising their Lord and convincing people to convert. One day, they came to Joni's house.

The Christian priest criticised the tribals and their religious beliefs harshly. "The tribals are backward and illiterate. Their religious beliefs are mere superstitions that push them to hell. Whereas Christianity is like pure water that washes away ignorance and superstitions and takes you closer to God."

Everyone listening to the priest was upset, but no one spoke out. They were scared. They didn't want to antagonise the priests because they were supported by the landlords. And nobody dared to antagonise the landlords!

But one young boy was not afraid of anyone! It was Birsa.

"No religion pushes anyone to hell! All religions take you to God. The one who calls any religious belief superstitious is ignorant!" he declared.

There was a stunned silence. The missionaries left.

Joni's father-in-law was very angry at Birsa's behaviour. "The same people might become our saviours tomorrow. How can we even think of antagonising them!"

As expected, Birsa's stay at Joni's place became very uncomfortable for everyone. He began spending more and more time outside the house, in the fields and forests. Among the trees and winding streams, Birsa felt a profound connection to the earth and its rhythms. He had developed an interest in playing the flute, which became his constant companion now.

One day, Birsa hurt his leg while cutting wood in the forest. Joni called the *ojha*, a local village healer, to have a look. The man saw Birsa's leg carefully and declared that he had been possessed by an angry evil spirit. A goat would have to be sacrificed in order to please the spirit and cure Birsa.

It was normal to sacrifice goats to make peace with the evil spirits, according to the Bongo tradition of the tribals.

As Joni was about to make arrangements for young Birsa's so-called treatment, he stopped her. His compassionate heart could not bear to even think about hurting a goat, let alone killing it.

Birsa's leg injury began to heal on its own, and he made a full recovery within a few days. This incident made him realise that the claims about evil spirits were mere superstition.

As he was growing, just like for the goat, young Birsa was becoming increasingly sensitive to the helplessness of the tribals as well. All around him, he observed their displacement from their own lands, their exploitation and financial hardships. The same was happening with his family too. It was just that now he could see and understand it better.

Unknown to him, the seeds of leadership and resilience were sown in him, preparing the 10-year-old Birsa for the challenges that lay ahead.

After completing his primary education, Birsa left Khatanga and went back to his parents.

3
Awakening to Injustice

Sugna and Karmi welcomed Birsa home with open arms. He had done well in primary school, making Sugna proud. The next step was to enrol Birsa in a missionary school for further studies.

Missionary schools only took Christian students, hence Birsa had to be converted.

Sugna wanted Birsa to study as much as possible, to have a better future. Embracing a new religion was the only way to do that. So, Birsa Munda was baptised to become Birsa David.

In those days, the German Christian Mission at Chaibasa was well known for running a high school. Birsa was enrolled there.

By now, Birsa had realised that he must study to learn the language of the colonial rulers to save the tribal lands from the British. But he couldn't have known the obstacles he would face on the path!

During his time at the missionary school, Birsa learned the English language, the aim and functioning of the mission, and of course the Christian prayers. It was a new world for him, and he enjoyed the structured process of learning. He spent whatever free time he had in the library.

Birsa found many interesting books to read, including the Bible. His heart could not agree with what the teachers taught in the class on religion—they always emphasised on the superiority of Christianity over all other religions. He wanted to understand the story of the man the missionaries worshipped, their Lord Jesus. When He taught that all were one in God's eyes, why then should his followers feel superior to others?

However much Birsa read about the trials and betrayals faced by Jesus and the miracles He performed, his heart still believed in and prayed to only his own God, Singbonga, the Sun, the creator of the universe.

The missionary school strictly followed the norms of Christianity, shielding the students from their tribal roots. But Birsa managed to stay connected to his own tribal culture. Even with so many restrictions, he mastered archery, swordsmanship and wrestling. Birsa loved music and became an expert flautist. It is said that when he played his flute, all birds and animals came out to listen to him.

Birsa had a good voice and sang tribal folk songs whenever he got a chance. Along with his flute, he also carried a tuila, a one-stringed instrument made from bamboo attached to a dried pumpkin resonator, everywhere with him. Like other children of his age, Birsa loved to dance as well.

Everything about the missionary school was great, except when they spoke highly about Christianity.

Though Christianity talked about equality, about loving your neighbours as yourself, yet Birsa noticed that the ways adopted by the missionaries in India were in total contradiction to their own teachings.

Birsa firmly believed that no religion teaches people to disrespect another religion. But the Christian missionaries disrespected the tribal religion. He could see the tribals being exploited all around him. He also realised that he was trapped, like all the other tribals.

Education was the only way to break out from the trap, so Birsa continued studying.

The first two years of Chaibasa changed him from the nervous boy who had accompanied his father to a confident teenager. As Birsa grew, he became more deeply aware of the injustices being faced by the tribals under the oppressive British rule.

The missionaries promised the tribals to get their lands back from the landlords if they embraced Christianity. For the tribals, the land was their mother, and they could give up their lives to protect it. The landlords had taken away their land by force and deceit. So, if embracing Christianity gave them the hope of reclaiming their lands, then it was a small price to pay. Or so the tribals thought.

Unfortunately, it was not so.

From one village to the next, the missionaries started converting the tribal families, promising them full support of the Church in getting their lands back from the landlords.

As was expected, the landlords refused to let go of the lands unless the British government compensated them adequately enough. And the British government had no such intention! Some of the landlords stopped funding the missionaries, which made them turn around and start appeasing them.

In this chaos, the tribals could see that getting their lands back was not going to be easy. All the promises made by the missionaries turned out to be false. The tribals were disappointed and angry. They wanted to convert back to their own faith. The tribal leaders, Munda Sardars, started warning the tribals to not be tempted anymore by the missionaries. The environment of Chaibasa became very tense.

Birsa's missionary school was no better! One day, in the prayer assembly, one of the priests started calling the tribals "uncivilised, ungrateful traitors, stuck in their superstitions".

Birsa could not tolerate this! He got up and shouted, "Mundas are not traitors! You are traitors! You are exploiting us with your lies. You promised to get us our lands back from the landlords. But you didn't do it. You are here only to convert us to your religion. We Mundas have seen through your lies and deceit. We know how to fight for our rights. You had better watch out!"

The priest was stunned as were others. The news of this confrontation spread like wildfire. Birsa's courageous words resulted in him getting expelled from the school but turned him into a local hero.

With the seeds of rebellion rooted firmly and growing strongly inside him, Birsa Munda left Chaibasa, heading back to his parents in Chalkad.

4
The Search

Sugna and Karmi had moved back to Chalkad a year back. Sugna was unable to find a regular job in Bamba.

Birsa was aware of this. But what he was not aware of was how much Chalkad had changed in the last decade. His childhood memory of the village was of friendly people. The landscape remained unchanged but there were no familiar or friendly faces anywhere. In fact, Birsa felt a kind of fear in the atmosphere.

Reaching home, it was soon clear to Birsa that he could not go back to that life anymore.

The atrocities of the landowners had increased. The Christian missionaries had fooled the tribals into conversion but had withdrawn all support after some time. The tribals were back to where they had started from, and in a much worse condition.

By now Birsa's sisters Daskir and Champa were married, his brother Komta was looking after their parents. Komta worked hard and yet barely managed to provide two meals for the family, just like Sugna did in his time. There was anger in Komta and helplessness in Sugna and both lived in fear of the landlords.

No, Birsa was not going to waste his life like this! He had anger too. But his anger led to his determination to bring about a change – seeking independence from the oppressors.

One night, 15-year-old Birsa left his home quietly. He walked away from his family, from Chalkad, into the wilderness. He wanted to be alone with his thoughts. He wanted to understand what he wanted to do and how to do it. He could not allow his own culture to be destroyed! By anyone!

Birsa wandered in the forests of Khunti and beyond, with no destination or plan in mind. The forest reminded him of his mother. He felt as though it was crying silently, pleading to be saved … something he had seen in his mother's eyes too.

The forests sustained, nourished, and protected the tribals since the beginning of time. The British administration had taken over the forests and was systematically destroying them to create agricultural land for themselves, inviting non-tribals to cultivate it.

The observations of injustice stirred something deep within Birsa's heart—a fierce determination to stand up for his people and defend their rights. He realised that he could not remain silent in the face of oppression, and resolved to act. But how?

Lost in these thoughts, he reached the village of Bandgaon, where the next chapter of his life was going to begin.

5
Learning and Introspection

Bandgaon was a peaceful village. Birsa decided to stay there for the time being. Jagmohan Pande, the landlord of Bandgaon, was a reasonable man.

Unknown to Birsa, his quest had ended. He met Anand Panre, a scholarly man, who worked as Jagmohan Pande's treasurer.

Anand had studied the Hindu scriptures in great depth. He had good knowledge about the Vedas, Puranas, Upanishads, *Ramayana*, *Mahabharata* and Bhagavad Gita. Birsa had found his guru!

Birsa lived with Anand Panre and looked after him like a disciple would do in a gurukul. Such was his zeal for learning! Not only scriptures, Anand taught his young student all about local plants and their healing properties. He also encouraged him to think and question. This was in such stark contrast to his education in the missionary school, Birsa often thought. He was finally on the right path to his ultimate mission.

In Anand Panre's company, Birsa began to appreciate Hindu philosophy and culture. He understood that to liberate the tribals from the British, he would first have to liberate them from Christianity. By accepting Christianity, they had turned their backs on the great traditions of their own ancestors. This had to be rectified.

Birsa also learned that the law of the land was meant to bring order in the society. And that it is fair to all. Everyone was equal in the eyes of law. This was an eye-opener! So far, Birsa had seen the landlords and the tribals being treated very differently by the so-called law.

Anand Panre had a huge collection of books, which he encouraged Birsa to read. Birsa recalled his days in the library of the missionary school in Chaibasa. He loved going through the books there too, but there was no one to help him understand them. Here in Bandgaon, his guru Anand Panre guided him patiently as he explored the books.

The Vedas taught him the secrets of Hindu philosophy, traditional medicine and even music. *Ramayana* taught him to work for the upliftment of the society and *Mahabharata* taught him to fight for his rights. The more he read the epics, the more Birsa felt convinced that he should fearlessly fight against the tyranny of the British. He also observed that Hindu scriptures never preached

hatred towards other religions, nor did they talk about converting.

Birsa was relieved that he did not have to leave his Singbonga to follow the path of Hinduism. This was very important because Singbonga played a very important role in his identity, the identity of Mundas. A person's identity is their source of strength. Birsa had realised this while staying with Anand Panre. He understood that as long as he remained true to himself and to the land that had nurtured him, he would always find his way home.

The atrocities of the landlords, the unfairness of the British administration, the abject poverty, had resulted in the tribals losing their identity. This was the reason why they were confused and lived in constant fear. They feared the missionaries who refused to help if they did not follow the diktats of Christianity. And in their hearts, they feared their own God when they did something totally contradictory to their traditional beliefs. For instance, they had to bury their dead as Christians and while doing that, they felt they were betraying their own God, according to whom they used to cremate the dead earlier. It was an extremely conflicted life that the converted tribals led.

After reading the Hindu scriptures Birsa gave up eating meat and fish. He started worshipping the tulsi plant and spoke vehemently about protecting and looking after cows. He started wearing saffron clothes and wooden sandals, and even the scared thread!

In the four years that he lived in Bandgaon, Birsa became quite popular with the village folk. He had grown into a strong and handsome young man with a gentle demeanour. The angst that he used to carry within him had been replaced by the peace of knowledge and understanding of the world.

Birsa used his knowledge of the herbs to heal people in the village. Though he was young, yet people respected him as a healer. They would come to him with all kinds of physical ailments, and while treating them with herbs Birsa would talk to them about their problems. Slowly, people realised that they could trust him to guide them on the right path.

Birsa was successful in bringing about the change in the mindset of the villagers. They trusted him when he told them to return to their traditional ways. Slowly but surely, Birsa was giving the lost strength of the tribals back to them.

This journey was not without its hurdles. There were

still a lot of superstitions in the people, belief in the evil eye and so on. Birsa had to patiently explain the principle of a single God as the creator and protector to the village people. Only that God could destroy, no other power could. Birsa also convinced people that to worship God, an animal need not be killed or sacrificed as an offering, grains were good enough!

Birsa would visit the neighbouring villages to help the tribals in any way he could. Once, smallpox struck in one of the villages he had visited. The local *ojha* spread the rumour that it was because of Birsa's visit that their gods were upset and punished the villagers with disease.

When Birsa went there again to help, the villagers stopped his entry, blaming him for the epidemic. However, the epidemic continued to worsen and the *ojha* was unable to do anything to contain it. When all the sacrifices failed, the villagers realised their mistake and rushed to Birsa. They apologised for their ignorance and requested him to help.

Birsa went back to the village and worked day and night, taking care of the sick. He would raise his hands in prayer and then treat the patients with herbs. Soon, people became well. The village got rid of not only smallpox but their superstitious belief in the *ojha* as well!

During his time at Bandgaon, Birsa had developed a habit of sitting alone for hours in quiet meditation. People who happened to see him sitting quietly, claimed to see

a glow around him. Word spread and people came to see him, talk to him, and went back happier. He not only healed people physically but healed them mentally as well. They started calling him "mahatma".

In looks too, Birsa stood apart from other Mundas. He was taller and fairer, and had bright intelligent eyes. It was no surprise that the Mundas started looking up to him as their God!

One day, an old lady came to visit Birsa. The moment she looked at him, she exclaimed that the lines on Birsa's forehead indicated that he was their prophet and was born to release them from the tyranny of the oppressors!

It was four years since Birsa had left Chalkad. Anand Panre felt that it was time Birsa returned home and told him so.

Nineteen-year-old Birsa started on yet another journey. This time he was going home.

6
Going Home

The Birsa who was returning home was a very different person from the Birsa who had run away from home four years ago. It was as though he had grown four decades in wisdom in the last four years!

Birsa's reputation of a healer had preceded him. So when he reached Chalkad, he was greeted by the Sarpanch of the village. It was a pleasant surprise for Birsa. His parents Sugna and Karmi cried tears of happiness to see their son alive and well.

Other than this, the condition of the village had not changed in these years. Birsa was happy being home but had yet to decide his course of action.

One day, he confided in his elder brother Komta that he wanted to help people but was not sure where to begin.

"The Sarpanch is doing it for you," Komta said with a smile, pointing at a group of people coming towards their hut. The Sarpanch had brought his close friends to meet Birsa, the healer. They had a child with them, who had high fever.

Birsa laid his hand on the child's head, chanted something and blew over his hand. Miraculously, the child's fever went down! Since people were poor, the only way they could pay back Birsa was through food. The child's mother had brought some vegetables with her, which she respectfully placed at Birsa's feet.

This started a trend. People would come to Birsa to get healed and leave some food behind.

After some time, Birsa started missing the moments of solitude that he enjoyed at Anand Panre's house. So he decided to build for himself a small mud hut, where

he would sit for a couple of hours, chanting. His family let him be, as they felt that Birsa probably needed to do that to maintain his healing powers.

The entire thing about Birsa's healing powers was still very mysterious and magical to everyone, especially to those who had known Birsa since birth.

Initially Birsa was also not too sure about his own healing powers, as to how he developed them. He had learnt a lot about medicinal herbs from Anand Panre and utilised that knowledge to treat people's ailments. But being able to heal without using any herbs was new, even to him!

One night, Birsa had a strange dream. He saw a grey-haired man sitting on a golden throne with a spear in his hand. There was a mahua tree in front of him and four people standing next to his throne. Birsa saw himself as one of the people, the others were a king, a judge and a spirit. The old man asked all four of them to get the treasure that could be seen on top of the mahua tree. The problem was that the tree was slippery. The spirit, the judge and the king could not climb the tree at all. Every

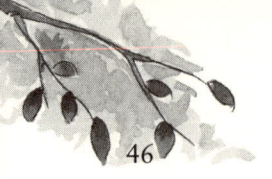

time they tried, they slipped. But Birsa could! He climbed up the slippery tree, brought down the treasure, and gave it to the old man sitting on the golden throne.

Suddenly, Birsa woke up and realised that the old man was Singbonga! The spirit represented the superstitions in the name of religion, the king symbolised the landlords, and the judge was the British government. Singbonga wanted Birsa to save his people from these three!

Birsa felt relieved. He had clarity now about where his duty lay. He had to follow the command of his God, Singbonga. So he decided to visit the village people personally. He sat with the families, talking to them about the harm the British rulers were causing through their Christian missionaries. He made them understand that their own identity as tribals was very important, as were their rights. They should proudly protect them, and fight with anyone who tried to force them to follow their religion.

Birsa quoted Krishna's discourse of Bhagavad Gita and told people the story of how Krishna helped the Pandavas win the war of *Mahabharata* against the oppressive Kauravas. Since he also played the flute like Krishna did, some of the people started looking up to Birsa as Krishna!

Wherever Birsa went, the tribals abandoned Christianity and returned to their original faith of worshipping *jungle* (forest), *jameen* (land) and *jal* (river). To that Birsa added *jantu* (animals) too.

Birsa had learnt patience from his guru Anand Panre. He patiently explained to people that it was better to worship one Singbonga rather than multiple gods. Slowly, he made them understand the uselessness of superstitions. He talked about having a tulsi plant in the house, and of the importance of personal hygiene as well as keeping surroundings clean.

From a healer, Birsa was now becoming a preacher. People came from far and near to listen to his talks. They would sit in the courtyard of his house to listen to his words of wisdom. When the number of people started increasing, Birsa shifted his seat to the fields, under a neem tree.

Birsa spoke about the Hindu epics and the practical wisdom they contained. People loved the stories he narrated from the *Hitopadesha*, *Ramayana* and *Mahabharata*.

His favourite story was about his interpretation of the Asur legend of the Mundas. It goes like this…

Seventy two epochs ago, in the *Kaliyuga*, sins had multiplied on *mrityuloka* (earth). Violence was rampant. Asurs (not to be confused with Hindu *asuras*) ruled the land. They were iron smelters, with furnaces blazing day and night. After some time, the heat of the furnaces started bothering God Singbonga in heaven.

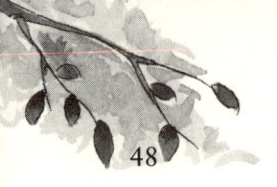

Singbonga sent a few birds as messengers to the Asurs, requesting them to light the furnaces only at one time, either during the day or during the night. The arrogant Asurs declared that they were the gods of earth and will do whatever they wanted. The furnaces continued to blaze.

Finally, Singbonga incarnated himself as a young boy Khasra Kora, whose body was covered with itchy sores and went down to earth. He went around to the Asur houses asking for work, but everyone turned him away.

There was an old childless Munda couple, who took pity on the boy and took him in. They fed him and looked after him as their own son. The boy started living with them and helped around the house. One day, a rooster ate the paddy that the boy had laid out for sunning. Unknown to others, the boy had miraculous powers. Using those, he filled up the couple's store with paddy.

Meanwhile, the iron smelting operations of the Asurs stopped abruptly. A wise man, probably an *ojha*, told them that unless they sacrificed a human, the iron will not begin smelting again. Fearing being chosen for sacrifice, everyone hid from the Asurs. Finally, the Asurs saw young Khasra Kora, who was living with the Mundas, and took him away.

A special furnace was built, and a number of rituals were performed, before the boy was put inside the furnace. The Asurs then blew air into the furnace continuously for three days. Finally, they did another set of rituals and opened the furnace. The boy came out glittering like gold, carrying with him precious gems! He told the Asurs that they should do the same and bring out the treasure that is kept within the furnace.

Driven by greed, the Asurs had furnaces built all over the land. All the Asurs, both young and old, entered these furnaces. When they cried as they were being burnt, Khasra Kora told their wives to blow harder, to help them look for the treasure. In three days, all the Asurs were burned to ashes. When their women asked for help, Khasra Kora rose in the air, heading towards heaven.

The Asur women clung to his legs, but he shook them off. The women fell on hills, high mountains, deep waters, dense woods and open fields and became their presiding spirits.

Birsa's followers started believing him to be Khasra Kora, an incarnation of Singbonga, who was especially sent to destroy the British who were like Asurs.

Birsa had studied Christianity in the missionary school, Hinduism from Anand Panre and his own Munda religion from his family, but he never condemned or promoted any religion. He picked up what he felt was the best from all religions and made it his own. His teachings came to be known as Birsait, and people started calling him Dharti Aaba or "Father of the Land".

Birsait encompassed the idea of one God, the creator, nurturer, and destroyer of universe. And that god was Singbonga, who did not require animals to be sacrificed for worship. A handful of grains was enough to worship him with. All superstitions were created by mischievous people and should be ignored. Cow, the provider of nourishment, was sacred and should be looked after properly. The tulsi plant was sacred and should be present and worshipped in every household. Meat, fish and liquor destroy the brain and should not be consumed. Food should be taken only after having a bath, and cleanliness of self and surroundings was essential to have a clear thinking.

Birsait also emphasised on loving each other and staying united as one big family, recommending one day a week to be devoted to prayer and meditation. Since Birsa was born on a Thursday, his followers made that the day for prayers.

Other than Birsa's soothing words, his miraculous deeds were also spreading far and wide. There was an instance when he sowed his own family's entire field with just a fistful of seeds. In another, he went to an epidemic struck village, and ordered the disease to leave through the main lane after making the sick people sit in a line on both sides of that lane. He got rid of the epidemic by just waving his sacred thread and chanting a mantra! People claimed that even animals like bulls would come and pay their respects to Birsa.

"Those who have complete faith in God are never left with any unfulfilled desires. They are satisfied even with little," Birsa would preach.

One day, a man got up from the gathering of Birsa's followers and questioned, "Can you prove what you are saying? Can you prove about being satisfied with little, if one has complete faith in God?"

Birsa smiled and gave the man a handful of rice, saying, "Sure, I can prove it. Pray to God with complete devotion and then cook this rice. God will fulfil your desire."

The man went home, prayed, and prepared the rice. The rice filled up the pot and was more than enough to feed his family of 11 members! There were many more such miracles experienced by Birsa's followers.

People wrote and sang songs about him and his miracles.

Birsa's popularity was not going well with the missionaries. They realised that whatever efforts they had put in to convert the tribals to Christians in the last few years were getting totally reversed in days and weeks! They had to fix this problem before it got out of hand.

Meanwhile, the wastelands of the villages were declared as forestland by the government. In the process, the ancestral rights of the forest-dwellers were taken away. A group of Munda Sardars opposed this and filed a petition in the court demanding restoration of their rights to grazing and firewood. The government ignored it.

Munda Sardars were trying to unite people against the British government's land laws but were not successful. They saw Birsa's popularity and decided to take his help.

The Sardars were fighting for land rights. It was a political movement. Birsa was fighting for the social reformation of the tribals. It was a social movement. Both had the common goal of tribal welfare.

The root of all the hardships of the tribals was their being rendered landless. Their ancestral land was taken away by the landlords, who were under the protection of the British government. The tribals were made to work like and treated as slaves. So it was important for them to get their land back.

Birsa agreed to join hands with Munda Sardars against their common enemy, the British rulers and the landlords. After all, he had to follow the command of Singbonga!

A new chapter in Birsa Munda's life had begun.

7
A Call to Action

Chalkad village became a famous place of pilgrimage as the tribals considered Birsa to be their God or Bhagwan. After all, who else could be so selfless in serving people, if not God! For them, as the sun was their God Singbonga above, so was Birsa their God below.

But this was not enough for the Munda Sardars. They wanted the warrior tribals also to follow Birsa. That was the only way they could create their own army against the British.

So the Munda Sardars started spreading fascinating stories about Birsa's miraculous powers. They said that Birsa could cure any disease and even give life to the dead! They encouraged the tribals to go to Birsa with all their problems, as he alone had all the solutions!

The message sank in and the tribals unanimously declared Birsa to be their messiah, their leader. They pledged their allegiance to him and vowed to even lay down their lives for him if need be. The plan of Munda Sardars was successful!

Birsa's following increased so much that the dais he had made so far to address people had to be replaced by a much larger space. The villagers happily cleared up a patch of land on the hill above Chalkad and built a couple of huts for Birsa and his family.

Seeing the speed at which things were changing in their lives after Birsa's return, Sugna and Karmi were in a permanent state of awe and gratitude. Like others, they also started addressing their son as Birsa Bhagwan. Komta was proud of his younger brother and always remained by his side.

People from more than 50 villages around Chalkad came to have *darshan* of Bhagwan Birsa Munda every day. The number of his followers increased steadily. Slowly, Birsa began to encourage them to resist the forces that sought to oppress them. He spoke against injustice at these gatherings, urging his people to unite and reclaim their dignity.

Birsa stressed on the fact that the landlords, priests and traders were outsiders. They were non-tribals. They were not to be trusted, as they took advantage of the honesty of the tribals. So was the case with the British administration that made laws helping the landlords to exploit the tribals. Birsa insisted that the tribal youths must be aware of their own rich cultural heritage. They must know the stories of the Kol and Tamar revolts to get inspired to fight for their own birthright.

Kols are the Kolarian indigenous people of India, comprising more than a dozen tribes. The Kols of Chota Nagpur region rebelled in 1831 against the economic exploitation of the tribals by the land tenure system introduced by the British, whereby landlords were created. The Tamar revolt was even before that, in 1782, by the tribals against their exploitation by the moneylenders.

Birsa told his people to make role models of the Santhal

brothers Sidhu and Kanhu, who took an oath to drive away the British from their homeland, leading a massive rebellion against them in 1855.

Meanwhile in Ranchi, the Christian missionaries and landlords were discussing ways to break Birsa's control over the tribals. The landlords spread false stories to malign his reputation, calling him fake and greedy. The tribals did not believe a word. They had witnessed Birsa's selfless service and healing powers themselves. For them, Birsa was their saviour. In fact, the landlords spreading rumours against Birsa resulted in increasing the tribals' hatred towards them.

Birsa took advantage of this hatred and united the tribals to form a huge movement. The movement had to be based on demands that they would present to the British government. Those demands, for the welfare of the tribals, were laid down carefully by Birsa.

He was very clear about the fact that the tribals should not be slaves to anyone. Since ancient times, the landlords and the upper castes had treated the tribals badly, making them work like slaves. This had to be stopped.

Birsa wanted the government to frame laws to protect the tribals from exploitation by the British, and to have provision to punish the landlords who exploited the tribals. Basically, he wanted everyone to be treated fairly, whether tribals or non-tribals.

The other important thing Birsa wanted was that the dominance of the landlords and upper castes over local forest reserves, land, mountains, and mineral resources should end. The tribals deserved an equal right to the natural resources.

Next was the issue of financial exploitation of the tribals. Birsa demanded that the tribals should get paid according to the work they did, and not less, as was happening. He also demanded that the land be made free from taxes, which meant no taxes to be given to either the landlords or the government.

Birsa wanted to be assured of the protection of tribal women, with the provision of strict punishment for those who misbehaved with them. He also wanted the tribal children to have the right to education and facilities for the same.

Birsa demanded that the tribals should not be treated as untouchables and should be allowed to visit temples and other religious places. They should have religious independence, and the Christian missionaries should not be allowed to convert the tribals to Christianity. There should be a law to see to it that the tribals are not forced to do anything that they did not want to.

Birsa's demands took care of all the issues faced by the tribals. They were so well thought out that after

Independence, the Indian Constitution made provisions for special laws to be framed for the welfare of the lower castes.

As more and more armed tribals gathered around Birsa, the British government feared a land movement accompanied by arson and chaos. They decided to take strict action against him. A police team was sent to Birsa's place in Chalkad, where by now, thousands of tribals had collected.

The moment Birsa came to know about his imminent arrest, he began motivating his people further.

"My brothers, we have suffered the tyranny of the British and the landlords for very long now. It's time we stopped doing so! These forests were cleared by our forefathers and turned into cultivable land. They rightfully belong to us. But the landlords have taken away our land and made us their slaves. We have lost our identity. We have lost our rights. Our children are going without food and our women are being mistreated by these tyrants. Enough is enough! Let's all unite and fight against the British and the landlords!"

Birsa's words fuelled the tribals and they were ready to face the police with their swords, bows and arrows. They had never protested earlier, but now with the police wanting to arrest Birsa, the tribals lost their patience

and retaliated fiercely. Led by Munda Sardars they were successful in making the police back off.

But the tribals were not satisfied. Their pent-up anger against the landlords burst out and they set fire to government offices. The landlords had to escape to save themselves. Finally, Birsa pacified them, convincing them not to waste their energy in destroying things.

Meanwhile, not only the police, even the British government was shaken by the show of aggression by the tribals. Something bigger had to be planned to nip the agitation in the bud, they felt. So, a series of charges were framed against Birsa that included serious crimes like obstruction of government work, arson, destruction of

government property, attacking policemen, and carrying out acts of violence.

An arrest warrant was issued against Birsa. More than a dozen policemen went to arrest him from his hut at night. Though Komta and his companions tried to put up a fight, they were no match for the armed police.

As he was leaving, Birsa told his people not to resort to any sort of violence, because the police was always better armed. There was no sense in getting killed. He promised to be back soon, to guide them towards their freedom.

Birsa was arrested and taken to Bandgaon. In that dark rainy night, the shoots of tribal revolution were growing fast, though hitherto unseen.

8
Birsa is Imprisoned

The news of Birsa's arrest spread like wildfire and people started gathering at Bandgaon. Seeing themselves surrounded by armed tribals, the police got nervous and called for more forces. In the quiet night,

under heavy guard, Birsa was shifted from Bandgaon to Ranchi prison.

The sky was overcast, and it was raining heavily. The moment Birsa entered the prison, one of its walls collapsed! This incident proved to the tribals that God was on their side, that their Bhagwan Birsa was right, and that he could not be imprisoned for long.

The administration decided to keep Birsa in prison till they collected enough proof against him to take him to court. This process was taking time.

Meanwhile, the anger among the tribals on the arrest of their Bhagwan was on the rise. They wanted to meet him, or at least see him, and they were willing to get killed by the police for doing so.

The British officers tried reasoning with them by saying, "Birsa is not God. He is as ordinary as you. If he were God, he could not have been arrested!"

The tribals were not convinced.

Finally, it was decided to try Birsa in court as soon as possible to show his vulnerability to his people. Little did the British know they were fighting a losing battle! Not a single tribal came forward as a witness against Birsa. All of them said that he was their spiritual leader and was not involved in any violence.

The British government finally charged Birsa with

misleading the tribals by claiming to possess extraordinary powers. He was spreading hatred against the British and encouraging his people to protest against them. Under the pretence of preaching his brand of religion Birsait, Birsa was turning his followers into armed warriors. By inciting people to not pay taxes, he was obstructing the government's functioning and committing treason.

The tribals stood by their leader. Every day for the three days that Birsa was brought to court, the number of his followers in and outside the court increased steadily.

They stood chanting his name and did not create any disturbance. Respecting their Bhagwan's wishes, the people did not carry any weapons.

Contrary to what the government had hoped for and believed, the trial turned 20-year-old old Birsa into a very powerful tribal leader.

Some government witnesses supported the allegations against Birsa, though nothing could be proved. The British were afraid that if Birsa was let free, it would lead to a larger movement with possibly catastrophic results. Hence, it was recommended that to teach him a lesson, Birsa should be punished severely. They wanted to set an example so that Birsa and his people do not dare to indulge in such activities in future.

The court sentenced Birsa to two years of imprisonment. He was sent to Hazaribagh prison to serve his sentence.

Following Birsa's arrest, the tribals had no leader to guide them. They could not sustain the movement on their own, so they went back to the daily grind of their lives. But the Munda Sardars tried their best to keep Birsait alive. They organised minor protests here and there, inciting people to protest against Birsa's imprisonment, urging the tribals to resume the movement on Birsa's release.

Encouraged, some of Birsa's disciples started spreading rumours like Birsa had disappeared from the prison, leaving behind a clay statue of himself! They declared that their leader was protected by God Singbonga who had chosen him to be the interpreter of his will.

With Birsa in prison, the British increased their atrocities on the tribals, fully supported by the landlords. As if this was not enough, the tribals had to face a terrible famine in 1896, with the worst hit areas being the regions following the Birsa movement. Crops were destroyed. Widespread poverty and hunger resulted in looting and killing.

But the landlords were not bothered. Their only concern was to destroy the identity of the tribals. They were determined not to let another revolt happen. The Christian missionaries, meanwhile, used this opportunity to help people by distributing free rations and giving loans to rebuild huts to those who embraced Christianity. Understandably, the tribals converted.

The British government continued to empower the landlords, and the Christian missionaries continued to convert. Squashed between these two forces, the condition of the tribals worsened each day.

The Munda Sardars started regrouping again. They started going from one village to the other to gather support. They assured the tribals that as soon as Birsa is freed, the movement would be launched again. This time it would be better managed, so that the British are compelled to listen to their demands.

By imprisoning Birsa, the British had won a small battle. They had not won the war yet. Instead, they had provided ammunition for a much bigger rebellion!

9
Birsa is Released

Birsa was released from prison in 1897. Two years of rigorous imprisonment would have broken anyone, but not Birsa. He walked out as calmly as he had walked in. But still waters run deep as they say. Behind the calm,

Birsa had become more determined than ever to selflessly fight for justice, to ensure that his people were treated fairly.

The news of Birsa's release spread from village to village. He was given an enthusiastic welcome by the eagerly awaiting people. Dancing and feasting went on for days to celebrate the homecoming of Bhagwan Birsa.

While the celebrations were going on, Birsa did not waste time and sat down with his companions to get an update of the situation. He was shocked to hear how the government had increased their oppression tactics on the tribals, and vowed to fight it. The only good news was that Munda Sardars had maintained their efforts to sustain the movement that he had started. So, at least, Birsa had something to build upon.

The preparations to oppose the tyranny of the British government and the landlords started afresh. This time it was with the strong underlying emotion that it was better to die fighting for their rights than dying in humiliation. This time the movement was more political than religious or social.

The revolutionaries were divided into three groups. The first group comprised the most trustworthy allies: a small group of 20 gurus or preachers, in whose houses Birsa's followers or Birsaites, as they were called now, held

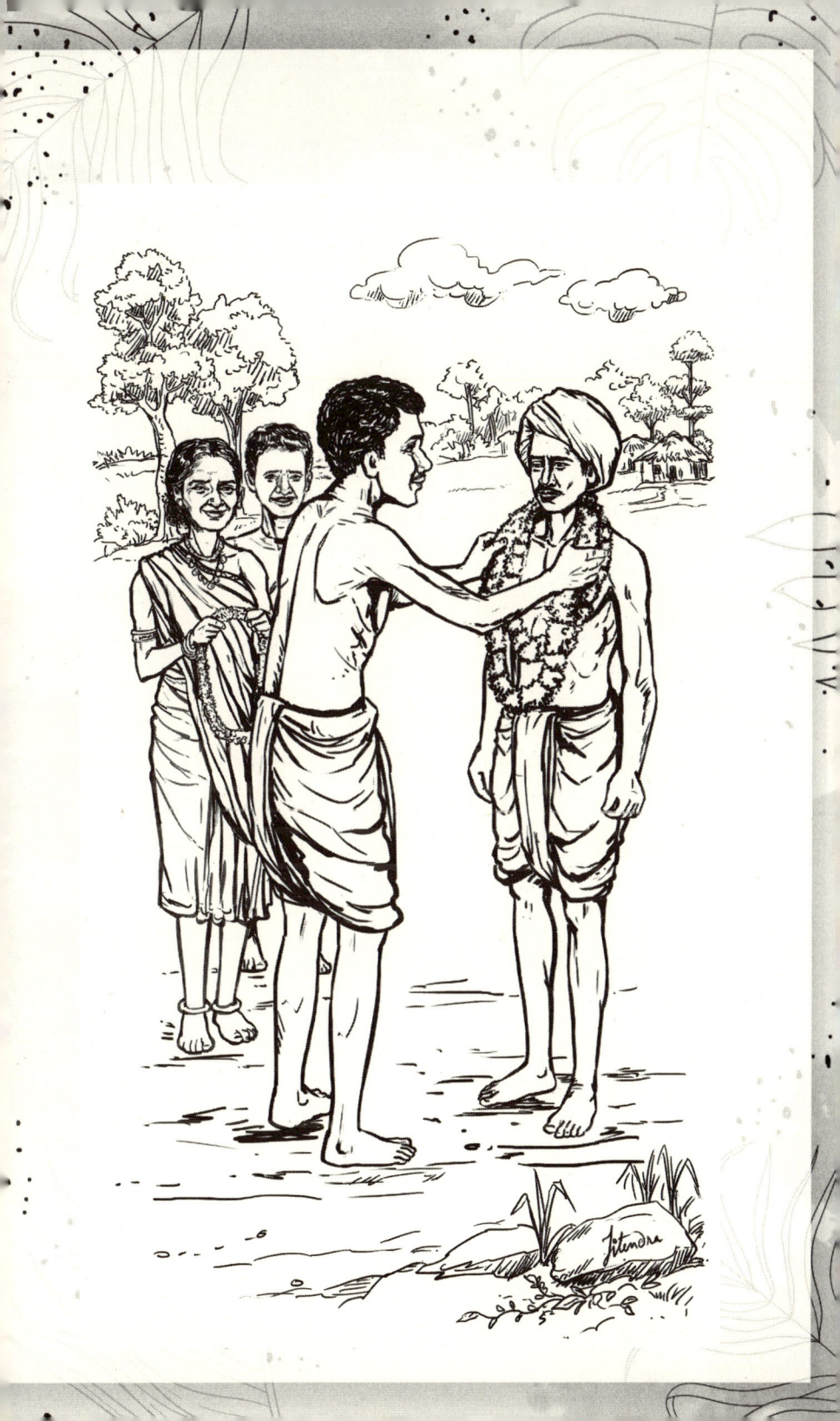

secret meetings every Thursday and Sunday. These houses were away from the main villages and provided a safe place to store weapons. Only Birsa and his close companions were allowed to enter them. The preachers also held the responsibility to continue teaching and reinforcing Birsa's religion, Birsait.

The second group of revolutionaries were the veterans who believed in fighting it out in the open. They were chosen very carefully from all over the country. The third group was of the new recruits who were not included in the meetings but were given specific responsibilities. They were the maximum in number and continued to increase steadily.

Birsa felt that their earlier movement was not as successful as he had wanted it to be, because of lack of management and control. This time, he wanted to involve the entire tribal community, and not just a few thousand Birsaites. He wanted a national movement, not a regional one.

Determined, Birsa decided to travel to reach out to fellow tribals in far-flung villages. The great uprising was about to begin.

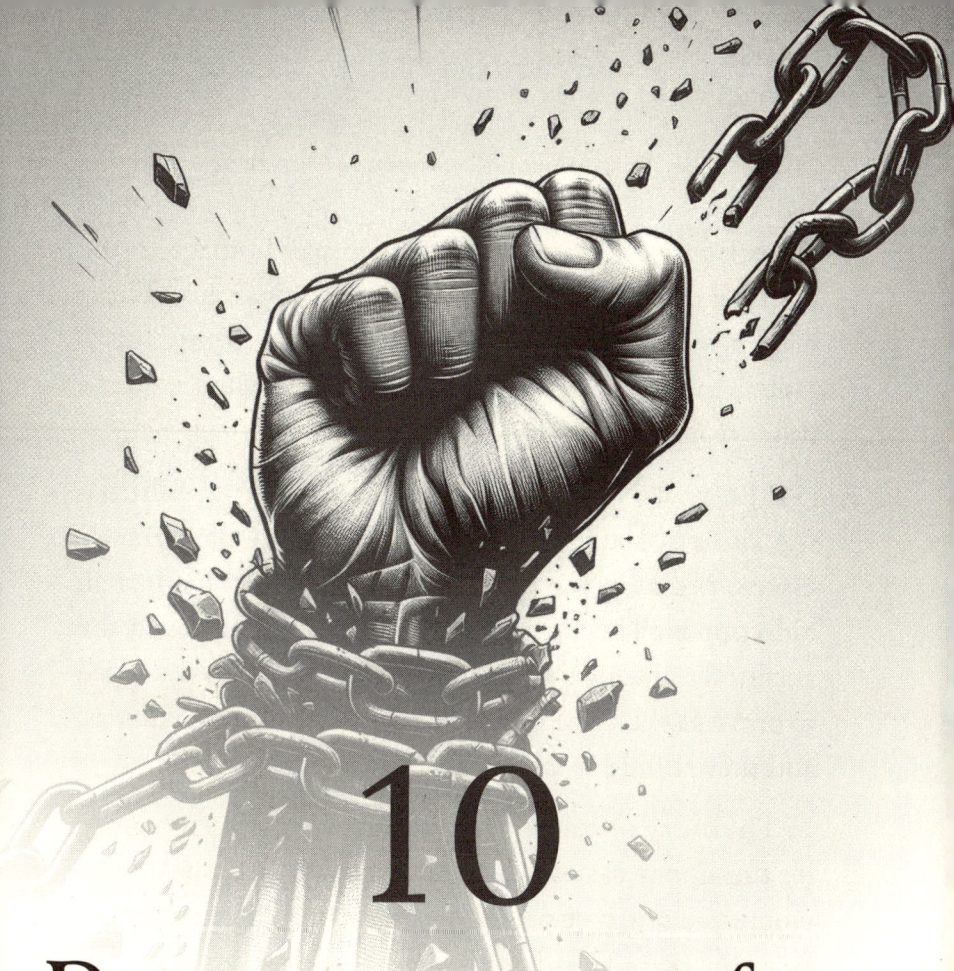

10
Preparations for the Uprising

Birsa decided to visit Chutia temple, Jagarnathpur (Jagannath Puri) temple and Navrattan fort, before embarking on the movement against the British. It is believed that these three places were built by the Mundas.

So Birsa felt it was important to pay homage to the ancestors of their race and take their blessings. These blessings were in the form of tulsi leaves from Chutia, sandal paste from Jagarnathpur and the sacred soil and water from Navrattan.

The most important reason for visiting Chutia, the site associated with the Chutia Purti clan, Birsa's direct ancestors, was a copper plate. The temple had an old copper plate, the inscription on which proved the ancestral rights of Mundas to worship there. Birsa wanted to prove to everyone that the temple was built by Mundas, and they should be allowed to enter it and worship.

The entry of tribals into the temple had been banned by the upper castes. Birsa always said that any temple where the entry of people was based on caste could not be an abode of God.

Since he knew that he was being observed by the British, Birsa took care and split his men into three groups, so as not to attract any attention. They reached the temple from three directions. They first prayed and then looked around for the copper plate. Birsa found it and they all celebrated their victory by singing and dancing. They also plucked leaves of the tulsi plants growing around the temple.

Their activities attracted the attention of the local villagers, but before they could do anything, Birsa and his men fled from there.

Preparations for the Uprising

This daring act of Birsa gave courage to the tribals to fight the upper castes. It was his first activity in public after his release from prison.

The British administration arrested a few tribals but released them once they claimed that they acted on Birsa's orders. Their sole motive was to show the people that the Chutia temple was an ancestral temple of the tribals.

An arrest warrant was issued for Birsa, but he could not be traced.

The visit to Jagarnathpur temple was not so dramatic. Birsa reached there with his companions and prayed. They smeared their foreheads with sandal paste and vowed to fight for their rights till death.

The Mundas believed that their ancestors came from all over the country to pray in the temple but later their entry was banned. Birsa wanted to break this ban too and make people aware of their own exploitation by the priests.

Birsa told his followers about the supernatural power of the water of Navrattan fort. Sprinkling that water on themselves would give them supernatural strength, which they needed to drive away their enemies, he said.

So, a large number of men, women, girls and boys accompanied Birsa. They filled the pots they were carrying

with them with water from Navrattan after performing religious rituals and tying the holy thread around their wrists. Birsa also collected some soil from that place.

The visits to these three places stirred the imagination of tribal people, reviving their past. The sacred relics of their ancient religion were secured. They had tulsi from Chutia, sandal paste from Jagarnathpur and sacred thread from Navrattan. They even had the holy water that would transform them into heroic warriors.

Physically, the tribals were ready anyway, their mental and psychological preparations for the revolt were also complete. Birsa went back to Chalkad to plan out the next steps.

Chalkad being Birsa's home, was also the hub of his movement. The British administration kept a close watch on him. Birsa and his family were practically surrounded by the police.

Since the movement was in full swing, with new people joining it every day, Birsa felt it was risky to run it from Chalkad. He decided to shift his base to Dombari.

This shift also marked the end of Birsa's prophet phase. Birsa was regarded as a freedom fighter now.

11
Call for Rebellion

Dombari was a quiet region surrounded by hills, opening into the valley of Domba. The terrain was familiar to Birsa and the tribals, but was not easily accessible to the government forces on short notice. The forests and the wild vegetation ensured enough food supply. Water was also in plenty. In short, it was the best and safest place for the revolutionaries.

Dombari was also the place from where the Kol mutiny of 1831-32 against the British began, so it had a sentimental value too. Tribals of that region included Mundas, Oraons, Hos and Bhumijas.

The first meeting of the representatives of Mundas from across the land was held at the house of Jagri Munda, in Dombari in February 1898.

Birsa always favoured non-violent means to resolve a conflict. He tried to convince the people to follow the non-violent path, giving the argument that whichever path they followed, it would take the same amount of time. But this time, the Munda Sardars were adamant. They were of the view that peaceful, legal methods would never be successful in their case. So to win the battle, they would have to resort to an armed rebellion.

Birsa pointed out that by taking the violent route, they would have to leave their families and children, give up

food, and possibly live in prisons. He also added that whatever method the people wanted to adopt, he would fully support them.

The tribals stuck to their stand of armed rebellion.

The next meeting was in March at Simbua Hill in Dombari. Over 300 armed tribals attended the meeting. It was the festival of Holi that day and they lit up a huge bonfire. Everyone sang and danced. The songs spoke about the fearlessness of the Mundas and paid tribute to the Kol rebellion.

Birsa declared that the British administration was like Ravana and had to be destroyed. They set fire to a plantain effigy as a symbol of their protest. Birsa tried one more time to explain the hardships associated with an armed revolt, but the Mundas were willing to sacrifice their lives to get freedom for their people.

The next meeting in Dombari was held in October. The tribals gathered with red and white flags. The white flags represented the tribals while the red flags represented the exploitation of the British government and the landlords.

Birsa stood on a high platform to address the gathering. He pitched a white flag in the east and a red one in the west, declaring that there would be a fight, and the ground would become red with the blood of their enemies.

"My dear brothers, we tribals have always led selfless lives. We never abandoned patience and tolerance even during extreme hardships. But our enemies took our tolerance as cowardice and exploited us. Today, we have decided to oppose them, fight them. We will prove to them that we tribals do not hesitate to take lives or give up our lives whenever necessary. We want justice at any cost and will not rest till we get it!"

With this, Birsa declared the beginning of an armed rebellion.

Many more secret meetings were held by Birsa at secluded spots all over Munda region at night. The Birsaites were told to gather weapons, make bows and arrows and sharpen their axes in preparation for the armed revolution called "Ungulan".

The local administration had failed to execute the warrant against Birsa after the Chutia incident. Ultimately it was given up, assuming that a little bit of song and dance to prove a point was not really harming anyone. It was not treason.

Most of Birsa's moonlight meetings on hilltops had songs and dances, which the British did not take seriously. Little did they know what sinister plans were brewing amidst song and dance! Had they bothered to listen carefully to the lyrics, they would have seen how Birsa

was instigating his people to destroy the colonial forces!

The Christian missionaries realised that Birsa was active when they saw a number of converted tribals abandoning Christianity and reverting to their old ways. The landlords also sensed that Birsa was up to something. But nobody had any proof of anything.

It was only after multiple incidents of burning plantain effigies came to light that the local police started paying attention. By this time they knew that Birsa had moved his base to Dombari, so they decided to control him by cutting his supplies from outside. The terrain of the region was too wild for the police to search in. The best course of action seemed to plug the entry to the region.

After some time, the Munda families started feeling the pressure. The food supplies were dwindling, and the children were starving. At this point, the Birsaites decided to loot the food stores of the churches. In order to save the lives of their own people, the Mundas did not hesitate to loot and burn the godowns and houses of the landlords and traders who had oppressed them. They did not kill anyone but destroyed the properties and used the loot to fund their movement and feed their own families. When they needed arms and ammunition or horses, they destroyed the police stations.

Birsa held the last meeting with 60 Birsaite gurus on 22 December 1899 in a cemetery. The general plan of action was decided, widespread riots on Christmas eve were discussed, preparations made, and responsibilities given to people according to their capabilities.

Birsa declared, "My brothers, we have tolerated enough exploitation by the British government and landlords. The time has come for us to unite and fight their corrupt practices. We have carried out several actions to show them our strength, and now we have to crush them! The clouds of slavery will clear soon, and the sun of freedom will rise, bringing happiness and prosperity for us. We must vow to shed every drop of our blood for the fulfilment of our mission. We must do or die! So, for the welfare of our own people, we will shed the blood of our enemies!"

Initially, the tribals tried not to kill anyone, but it became difficult to control so many of them. Those who had personal grudges because their family members had been killed, took the first opportunity they got to pay back by killing the killers.

During these last years of secret meetings and preparations, the Birsa movement had changed a lot. It began as a socio-religious movement using religious means to put their point across, to restore their dignity. But soon, the movement became political, using violence as the means to rebel.

After hesitating for a while, Birsa had given in to the Munda Sardars' strategies for the movement. Both needed each other. The Sardars needed a leader like Birsa, and he needed their support in terms of numbers. It worked because they had the common goal of fighting for freedom from the British rule.

12
The Uprising

Birsa declared that they would launch their movement on 24 December 1899. It was Christmas Eve, and the British would be busy with their families.

The British officers had an idea about Birsa's plans through the landlords' informers, but in the absence of any reliable information, they shrugged it off as a rumour. It was not unusual, because there were many rumours about Birsa, about his disappearing and appearing, about his superhuman strength, about his claims of enemy guns and bullets turning to water when facing Birsaites and so on.

The British administration considered Birsa to be more of an irritant than a threat.

The first phase of the Munda attack began as scheduled. The tribals created mayhem in Khunti, Chakradharpur, Karra, Basia, Torpa, Tamar, Ulihatu, Marcha, Kajara and other districts of Ranchi and Singhbhum by attacking the churches with poisonous arrows and balls of burning rags. People singing Christmas carols panicked and ran to save their lives. Many churches and police stations were burnt down.

Birsa always maintained that he had nothing against the religion of Christianity or any other religion for that matter, because all religions guide people on the path to God. He had problems with the institutions that forced people to convert to their religion. His aim was to fight for the rights of the tribals. The revolution was aimed to jolt the British government.

Unfortunately for Birsa, his movement was not his alone anymore. It had sprouted branches that were acting independently. There was a lot of pent-up rage in the tribals, which exploded in the form of killing missionaries, priests, moneylenders and landlords – basically their oppressors. The rebellion had turned into a war.

As expected, the repercussions were widespread.

The British government was on full alert, increasing their vigil across Singhbhum, Khunti and Ranchi. They made Bandgaon the main centre for their armed forces. The villagers were made to bear their expenses. The British thought that this might break the will of the poor villagers, but they were disappointed.

All efforts of the administration to trace Birsa were unsuccessful. The British could see how united the tribals were this time.

Birsa and his men lay low. The period of 26 December 1899 to 5 January 1900 seemed calm but was far from so. The rebels were preparing themselves for the next phase of attack.

The Munda attack had shaken up the Christian Mundas too. They had to be brought back to the fold.

Birsa appealed to all the tribals, "The British government is our enemy. It is the enemy of all the tribals. It is because of their exploitation that we had to pick up arms. All Mundas should support us, as we are fighting for all of us. By fighting the enemy together, we have a better chance of getting justice."

The appeal had the desired effect. All tribals including Christian Mundas understood that Birsa was fighting for a common goal, for their birthright. As a result, all tribals joined hands with the rebels.

For the second phase, Birsa's strategy was to clash directly with the authorities. This time there would be no attack on the churches.

Sardar Gaya Munda was one of Birsa's most trusted companions. On 5 January 1900, a secret meeting was organised at his house in Etkedih. About 60 rebels were present at the meeting. Unfortunately, the police came to know about it, and they surrounded the area.

A true warrior, Gaya decided to confront the enemy. He took the rebels to river Tajna. The men were armed with axes, swords, bows and arrows. Some of them sat on a large boulder on the riverbank, some washed their weapons, all waiting patiently for the police.

Meanwhile, the police was directed towards the river by the womenfolk of the village. The moment they reached the river, Gaya saw them and shouted, "The Sambhar deer have arrived! Kill them!"

The sudden attack stunned the police. They could not hold out against the tribals for long. Some policemen died, others fled.

When Gaya and his men returned home, they were greeted by songs of victory.

Next day, on 6 January, the Deputy Commissioner rushed to Gaya Munda's house with his men. Gaya had to be taught a lesson, they felt.

The police surrounded his house, ordering Gaya to come out. Why would he? Gaya stood at his doorstep and shouted back that it was his house, and the British had no right to enter it. The Deputy Commissioner knew

that going inside Gaya's house would mean certain death for himself and his men, so he kept on threatening from outside. He fired a few shots in the air, hoping to scare Gaya's family, but in vain.

While this was going on, the police got to know that more than 100 rebels had entered the forests surrounding the village and could soon come to Gaya's rescue. The Deputy Commissioner did not want that. He also did not want to shoot or use bayonets indiscriminately, as there were women and children inside the house. So, he ordered his men to set fire to Gaya's house.

As expected, Gaya's family came rushing out. All of them were armed with canes, scythes, axes and swords. The Deputy Commissioner fired at Gaya's shoulder to injure him. This helped the police in catching Gaya, but not before the Deputy Commissioner getting hit on the head by a cane struck by Gaya's wife!

This incident highlighted the deep hatred towards the British and the spirit of stubbornness in the tribals, including their women. It was very encouraging for the Mundas, while the British administration, in panic, declared a high alert situation and increased the security of churches and Christian missions across the affected regions.

During this time, at another meeting of the rebels at Bortodih, it was decided that their next target would be Khunti.

The Uprising

On the morning of 7 January, 300 rebel Mundas arrived, armed with bows and arrows, swords and shields, at the Khunti police station, which was a symbol of authority in the heart of Munda land. The policemen were caught unawares. At the time of attack, there were only five men and two guns in the police station.

The policemen opened fire, but the raging rebels were neither hurt nor discouraged. They continued pelting stones and shooting arrows. One of the policemen was killed, the others managed to escape when the tribals set fire to the police station. The rebels did not take the money, and even set the police horses free! They only wanted to destroy authority.

Khunti was in panic. People expected to be attacked at any moment. Terrified Christians took refuge in the church and the mission.

But nothing of that kind happened. The rebels were following their plan of clashing only with the authorities and not the church.

The ferocity of the Khunti attack was a nasty jolt to the British. Rumours began to spread that Ranchi would be the next target of the rebels on 7 January. As a result, armed guards were deployed to patrol the roads leading to the town. Hundreds of soldiers from other places were swiftly brought in for the protection of the town and its people. The threat to Ranchi, however, did not materialise.

British troops began to search for the rebels. They received information that the rebels might be meeting in Burju. The high officials of police and army reached there. It was already known that the rebels used Saiko valley, six miles from Burju, very frequently.

Police forces were also deployed in Bandgaon, Baring, Kundrugutu, Lagra, Sangra, Girga and Dorka, as these places were considered as Munda strongholds.

With all the extensive security arrangements in place, the British were ready to handle the rebel attack. But the anticipated attack on 8 January did not happen.

13
The Beginning of the End

A little away from Dombari and three miles north of Saiko was the Sael Rakab hill. It was surrounded by deep ravines and dense forests on three sides, with only a narrow path to approach from one side. The entire hill was dotted with caves where the tribals had moved in after Birsa movement's first attack of rebellion on 24 December.

The jagged stony sides of the hill were quite steep, but the tribals were used to tough terrains. They felt safe with their families in the Sael Rakab caves. Little did they know that that safety would be short-lived.

Birsa and his companions stocked up some of the caves with stones to be used as weapons, slingshots, axes, swords, bows and arrows, as well as food and clothing. They knew that sooner or later the British administration will discover their hideout. The rebels had caused enough havoc to ensure that!

The Mundas were right. The police force reached Sael Rakab on 9 January morning headed by the Commissioner and Deputy Commissioner. The force split into two, one unit climbing up the hill and the other moving to the far side of the hill to stop anyone from trying to escape.

The rebels spotted the police and started attacking them with stones and arrows. Many policemen were injured, and some died as well. The police stopped moving and invited the Mundas to have a dialogue with them. They wanted only Birsa to surrender and offered a reward for that.

The rebels refused the offer outright and told the British to surrender instead and leave them and their land in peace!

Finally, the police rushed up the hill from two sides, firing at the defiant rebels, who retaliated with stones and arrows. The rebels who fell dead were instantly being replaced by more. Their stocks of arrows and stones were diminishing fast but not their courage.

It turned out to be a bloodbath. Out of the 2,000 tribals who were in Sael Rakab that fateful day, 400 were killed by sunset.

On reaching the top, the police found that the rebels had escaped and only women and children were left in the caves. The families were taken captive with the hope to get information about Birsa out of them, but in vain. So, they were let off with a stern warning against helping Birsa and his movement.

The bodies of the dead Mundas were collectively buried in two large pits at Sael Rakab itself.

Birsa had eluded the British forces yet again. The moment they saw the police approaching, Birsa's companions convinced him to leave. They had enough

men and women to fight. They needed their Bhagwan alive to lead them.

From Sael Rakab Birsa went to Bortodih and from there to Ayubhatu. He had to continue to be on the run as the police and army were looking for him.

After the battle of Sael Rakab, the British administration was under the impression that they were successful in bringing the Birsa movement to a grinding halt. On 10 January, they launched a massive manhunt for Birsa.

The police searched through all villages, forests and hills of the region, however remote or inaccessible, and arrested those who they thought were Birsaites. Women and children were picked up and tortured for information. The Commissioner and Deputy Commissioner personally oversaw the operations and announced an award of Rs 500 to whoever helped them in finding Birsa. They also declared that those who gave information about Birsa, leading to his arrest, will be exempt from all taxes forever.

On 16 January, the headquarters of the rebellion, the villages of Rogoto, Sentra, Kotagara were raided. The men escaped. Their families were made prisoners.

On 19 January, the police got information that Birsa was hiding in the neighbouring Hesadih hill. All the villages in that area were raided and an abandoned hut was discovered.

The hut was clean and looked as though someone had recently lived there. Tulsi plants grew at the back of the hut and the fire in the kitchen was still warm. It was obvious that it was Birsa's regular hideout, and he had fled in the nick of time, yet again!

The British troops began confiscating the property of those associated with Birsa. Since the men had fled leaving behind their families, the women were not allowed to leave the villages. The routes used by the rebels to bring rations were blocked. Every day some Birsaites were arrested and tortured. Finally, the harassment worked, and the rebels captured on 21 January were willing to help the administration.

The converted tribals who had abandoned Christianity, embraced it again to escape the torture of the British. The tribals who helped the administration in getting the rebels arrested, were not only spared of exploitation, but were also rewarded. Seeing this, most of the rebels surrendered.

On 28 January, Birsa's close companions, Munda Sardars Donka and Majhia also surrendered. With that, the British government finally managed to end the Birsa movement that had, by now, spread over an area of about 400 square miles.

14
Birsa's Arrest and Final Days

Birsa was still elusive to the British. He was hiding in the forests near the village of Rogoto. He had not lost hope yet. He tried to round up the tribals once more to fight for their rights. He still talked about his religion, Birsait, to his loyal followers.

Not all of his followers were loyal though. Unfortunately, the money that the British administration was offering was successful in fanning the greed of people. Seven men from the villages of Manmaru and Jarikel succumbed to the temptation of the promised rewards. They decided to look for Birsa.

On 3 February, the men saw the smoke of a campfire in the deep forests near Sentra. On further exploration, they spotted Birsa sharpening his sword. Aware of Birsa's strength, the men waited till night. Once they were sure that Birsa was asleep, they first stole his sword and then pounced on him.

Although he put up a strong fight, the men managed to overpower an unarmed Birsa. The captors immediately handed him over to the Deputy Commissioner at Bandgaon, in return for their reward of Rs 500. Ironically, these seven men were tribals for whose rights Birsa was fighting.

Birsa was swiftly taken to Ranchi through a longer than usual route to avoid getting mobbed. But news of his arrest had spread already, and crowds gathered all along the way to have a glimpse of their Bhagwan.

In Ranchi too, rows of people stood on both sides of the streets to greet their Bhagwan Birsa, who despite being bound in chains smiled at them. Who else could behave like this if not God!

Birsa was happy to see that his efforts were not wasted. His fellow tribals were now aware of the unfair treatment meted out to them by the British. They had learnt to raise their voice and fight for their rights. The movement started by him would continue even after his death, of that he was certain.

Four hundred of Birsa's followers were imprisoned in Ranchi prison. He had to save them. So at the first chance he got, he told them to deny knowing him and that he would do the same.

Birsa was tried in the court like an ordinary man, on charges of loot, arson and murder. Deemed dangerous, he was put in solitary confinement. With hundreds of tribals in the prison, the administration did not want to take any chances of Birsa leading them into mutiny.

As usual, the court proceedings were taking time. And months of solitary confinement were taking their toll on Birsa's health.

On the morning of 30 May, Birsa could not eat the food given to him. It was not thought of as unusual because he had refused to eat earlier too. Since he was not complaining of being unwell, he was taken to the court for his usual hearing.

In the court, Birsa suddenly took ill and was taken back to the prison. On examination, his pulse was found to be feeble. Birsa's condition was deteriorating fast, his eyes had sunk in, and his voice had become hoarse. He looked like a bag of bones!

On 1 June, the Deputy Commissioner was told that Birsa had cholera and would not pull through. The prison doctor gave him medication, that helped briefly. But on 8 June, Birsa's condition worsened. Severe diarrhoea and vomiting had drained him completely.

Birsa's Arrest and Final Days

On the morning of 9 June 1900, 25-year-old Birsa started vomiting blood, and by 9 a.m., he passed away.

In order to avoid any uncontrollable violence from the tribals, the prison authorities got Birsa's body secretly cremated on the banks of river Harmu (a tributary of Subarnarekha), near the present Ranchi distillery.

Later, it was reported that the only case of cholera reported from the Ranchi prison was that of a criminal who had died 10 days before Birsa fell ill. All the other prisoners were in perfect health. How Birsa contracted cholera was a mystery!

Finally, on 10 June, on the basis of the prison doctor's statement, the state government affirmed that Birsa had died of cholera, which would not have been fatal had he not become weak from dysentery. However, Birsa's followers did not believe the official story. They accused that he was poisoned slowly to death by the prison administration.

The trial of the rebels lasted for a year. The British government successfully implemented their policy of divide and rule, resulting in turning some tribals into government witnesses. As expected, the verdict was given in favour of the government. Some rebels were sentenced to death and others to life imprisonment.

This finally marked the end of the Birsa movement.

15
Birsa's Legacy

Birsa Munda emerged as a prophet against the background of a disintegrating tribal socio-economic system in the latter half of the nineteenth century. Under the British rule, the tribals were deprived of their basic human rights, the minimum necessities of life, and were victims of severe exploitation.

The grabbing of Munda land by the people in power, the land that their ancestors had reclaimed from tigers and snakes, inspired their leaders, the Sardars to make efforts to recover what was rightfully theirs.

Birsa Munda was pursuing a similar goal, the difference being an extra socio-religious context added to it. He wanted to establish a tribal society that was unaffected by any non-tribal outside influences, one that followed its own golden past. To achieve that, all the enemies of their tribe had to be expelled. He planned a complete reconstruction of tribal life, by mixing the best of Hindu and Christian elements with the original tribal culture. Even during the second phase of his movement, which was more political than religious, Birsa continued to promote and propagate his idea of religion, which was called Birsait.

Birsa and his close companions composed prayers as a means to communicate Birsa's ideas. In their meetings, they sang these compositions, which were strung together in a bhajan melody. They sounded like bhajans or even Christian hymns.

The month old, short-lived tribal uprising under the leadership of Birsa Munda was filled with a passionate self-defensive need. For the first time since the Kol rebellion, the widespread deep-rooted feelings of anger against the injustices meted out to them was demonstrated by the Mundas.

The tribals' helplessness of fighting with their backs to the wall was used by Birsa to strengthen their resolve to break free from oppression; to salvage whatever they could and recreate their old world by all possible means.

The two incidents of the Gaya Munda encounter at Etkedih and the group resistance at Sael Rakab displayed the spirit of defiance and utter contempt for the British. They also showed the absolute faith in Birsa's leadership of the tribals. Despite facing adversity, Birsa remained steadfast in his commitment to the cause, inspiring hope and courage among his followers.

More than any other movement in the 19th century, the Birsa movement jolted the British administration into seeing the tribal issues, to which they had been deliberately blind thus far. A significant result was the abolition of Beth Begari or the system of forced labour that was earlier applied on tribals.

In 1902 the Gumla sub-division was set up for the authorities to keep a close watch on the relations between landlords and tribals. The administration of justice was quicker, and people were spared the trouble and expense of a long journey to Ranchi. Similarly, the Khunti sub-division was set up in 1905, to bring the seat of administration in the heart of Munda land.

Another important result of the movement was that

the British administration now understood the need for preparing a record of rights for the lands of Mundas.

Under the Chota Nagpur Tenancy Act of 1908, the legal rights of forest dwellers of Chota Nagpur region were finally reinstated. It was indeed the fruit of Birsa's relentless struggle and sacrifice!

Birsa Munda was identified with the aspirations of his people. He played an important role in awakening the tribals of not only Chota Nagpur but all across the country, inspiring them to fight against the injustice of the rulers. Birsa was not only a freedom fighter but was also a social reformer. Tribals believed in all kinds of superstitions and black magic. Birsa helped his people to get rid of these beliefs.

In 1940, the Indian National Congress and Forward Bloc observed Birsa Divas and named the main gate of their Ramgarh session as Birsa Gate.

Some followers of Birsa Munda later on joined Mahatma Gandhi in the struggle for freedom. Many tribes united to form Kisan Sabha, which also took part in the Indian freedom struggle very enthusiastically.

On 15 November 2000, on Birsa Munda's 125th birth anniversary, the then Prime Minister of India Atal Bihari Vajpayee created the state of Jharkhand as a tribute to the tribal population of the region. Jharkhand was carved out from the southern districts of Bihar including the Chota

Nagpur region and the Saranda Sal forest. Jharkhand means the land of forest.

On 10 November 2021, the Government of India declared 15 November, Birsa Munda's birthday, to be celebrated as Janjatiya Gaurav Divas to commemorate his contribution to the Indian freedom movement.

Birsa Munda is remembered as a hero and a visionary, whose unwavering dedication to his people paved the way for their empowerment and liberation. His story serves as a reminder of the power of one individual to ignite change, and challenge the status quo.

Although Birsa's life was cut short at a young age, his legacy lives on as a symbol of resistance and liberation; his courageous actions inspiring future generations to continue the struggle for justice and equality for indigenous communities.

It will not be wrong to say that the story of India, the story of the Indian freedom movement cannot be complete till we include the stories of the Indian tribal movements in it.

References

Kunwar, Gopi Krishna. *The Life and Times of Birsa Munda*. New Delhi: Prabhat Prakashan, 2021.

Law, Bimala Churn. *Tribes in Ancient India*. Poona: Bhandarkar Oriental Research Institute, 1943.

Leuva, K. K. *The Asur: A Study of Primitive Iron-Smelters*. New Delhi: Bharatiya Adimjati Sevak Sangh, 1963.

Roy, Sarat Chandra. *The Mundas and Their Country*. Calcutta: The Kuntaline Press, 1912.

Singh, K. S. *Birsa Munda and His Movement 1874-1901: A Study of a Millenarian Movement in Chotanagpur*. New Delhi: Oxford University Press, 1983.

Sinha, Tuhin A. and Ankita Verma. *The Legend of Birsa Munda*. Bhopal: Amaryllis, 2022.

Notes

OTHER BOOKS IN THIS SERIES

RANI GAIDINLIU

The fearless Naga chieftain was renowned for leading a heroic armed uprising against the British.

TILKA MAJHI

A trailblazer for the Adivasi community of Bihar, Tilka Majhi rallied the Santal people, training them as an army armed with bows and arrows to defend their land and heritage.

GURU GOVINDGIRI

A visionary social reformer and leader of the Bhil community living across Rajasthan, Gujarat and Madhya Pradesh, Guru Govindgiri stood firm against British oppression, demanding tax reforms and the abolition of forced labour.